Original Intent?

An essay on Article VI of the Constitution

By
Paul K. Blair

April 2008
Second Printing

Direct Inquiries To:

Paul K. Blair
1230 North Sooner Road
Edmond, Oklahoma 73034
E-Mail: pblair@fairviewbaptistedmond.org

ISBN 978-1-60643-257-0

Table of Contents

SECTION 1: Introduction

Recently, I had written a series of letters and sent them to some members of our U.S. Senate and Congress, expressing concern over the use of the Koran by newly elected Minnesota Representative Keith Ellison to take his oath of public office.

One response - by a fine committed member of our legislature, a solid Born Again believer in Jesus Christ who has consistently demonstrated his statesmanship and patriotism while in office -agreed with me in principle, but defended Ellison's actions as being protected by Article VI of the Constitution which states: *"The Senators and Representatives before mentioned... shall be bound by Oath or Affirmation, to support this Constitution; but no religious Test shall ever be required as a Qualification to any Office or public Trust under the United States."*

Grieved to hear that a dear friend and one of America's finest legislators has drunk the "kool-aide" of "reinterpretation" – I hope to put to rest this modern misconception in the pages of this short essay.

Karl Marx, the father of modern Communism, was quoted to say, *"A people without a heritage are easily persuaded."*

Certainly the secularist recognizes this to be true as in George Orwell's book *1984*, Big Brother was able to control the masses by the redefinition of words and the rewriting of history.

Christians also should recognize the seriousness of this as God repeatedly taught the Hebrew people to remember who they were as a people and who God was.

In Deuteronomy 6:10-12, God warned them that when they were in the Promised Land and they dwelt in safety and their pots were full of the harvest, not to become arrogant and forget the LORD, *"Beware lest you forget the LORD which brought thee out of the land of Egypt"*.

The Passover was a one time event in Israel's history. However, the Passover Feast was held annually to serve as "a memorial" (Exodus 12:14) in order to remember the LORD their Redeemer.

The knots and tassels in their prayer shawls were specifically designed for the purpose that every time they looked at them *"That ye may remember, and do all my commandments, and be holy unto your God,"* (Numbers 15:40).

After the crossing of the River Jordan the Hebrews were instructed to take twelve stones out of the middle of the riverbed and place them as a Memorial Marker in the Promised Land to **REMEMBER THE LORD YOUR GOD** and **REMEMBER YOU ARE HIS PEOPLE**, *"...and these stones shall be for a memorial unto the children of Israel forever."* (Joshua 4:7)

As a student of the Bible, I am convinced that America does not play a prominent role in the latter days. However, my prayer and effort is that America will remain strong until the Lord comes and calls His Bride home.

Certainly, all hell will break loose on this earth during those following seven years, but I pray that America will not become a hell on earth prior to the Rapture of the Church.

If we have a hope of surviving as a Republic, then we need to stuff the political correctness right away and recognize who we are as a people.

Well, who are we?

SECTION 2: Who We Were

Patricia Banomi, Professor Emeritus of New York University, in an article entitled *The Middle Colonies as the Birthplace of American Religious Pluralism* stated that, *"The colonists were about 98 percent Protestant."*

Christian historian David Barton notes that 98.4% of the colonists at the time of the signing of the Declaration were Protestant and 1.4% were Catholic.

Consider the roots of these Colonists as you read the constitution of the New England Confederation, May 19, 1643, *"Whereas we all came to these parts of America with the same end and aim, namely to advance the kingdom of our Lord Jesus Christ and to enjoy the liberties of the Gospel thereof with purities and peace, and for preserving and propagating the truth and liberties of the gospel..."*

Consider this diary entry made on February 22, 1756, by a 20 year old John Adams as to his vision of a "Eutopian Nation" (sic): *"Suppose a nation in some distant Region should take the Bible for their only law Book, and every member should regulate his conduct by the precepts there exhibited! Every member would be obliged in conscience, to temperance, frugality, and   industry; to justice, kindness, and charity towards his fellow men; and to piety, love, and reverence toward Almighty God...What a Eutopia, what a Paradise would this region be (sic)."*

Consider the Constitution of Delaware (1776):
ARTICLE 22: Every person who shall be chosen a

member of either house, or appointed to any office of place of trust, before taking his seat or entering upon the execution of his office, shall…make and subscribe the following declaration, to wit:

"I, ____, do profess faith in God the Father, and in Jesus Christ His only Son, and in the Holy Ghost, one God, Blessed forevermore; and I do acknowledge the Holy Scriptures of the Old and New Testament to be given by Divine inspiration."

Consider the Constitution of Pennsylvania (1776): Section 10: *And each member, before he takes his seat shall make and subscribe the following declaration, viz: "I do believe in one God, the Creator and Governor of the Universe, the Rewarder of the good and Punisher of the wicked. And I do acknowledge the Scriptures of the Old and New Testament to be given by Divine Inspiration. And <u>no further or other religious test</u> shall ever hereafter be required of any civil officer of magistrate in this State.*

Noah Webster, who compiled the Webster's Dictionary and wrote the first public school history book in 1835, entitled *"Republican Government"* **said this,** *" It is the sincere desire of the writer that our citizens should early understand that the genuine source of correct republican principles is the Bible, particularly the New Testament or the Christian Religion."*

Our Founding Fathers recognized that a man must be restrained from within or constrained from without. They knew that Liberty was only found in the Bible and the success of this American Experiment in government was dependent upon those Biblical values inculcated into the hearts and minds of its Citizens.

The future well being of America is fully dependent upon our rediscovering those "12 stones over Jordan" and remembering who we are and upon Whom we are founded or we will suffer the same fate as Israel who did not heed God's warnings.

SECTION 3: What Has Happened?

Over time, definitions have changed. For example, 50 years ago, the word "blue" meant a color, not an emotion. "Gay" meant happy, not what it has been misconstrued to mean in our day.

We run into problems today in that we apply 21st Century definitions and political correctness to 18th Century documents and we come up with an entirely different meaning.

Consider the definition of the word "religion." In Webster's 1828 Dictionary – after giving the comprehensive definition of the word, then referencing from the New Testament in the Book of James, Chapter One as an example of the practice of religion, Noah Webster actually differentiated between TRUE religion and FALSE religion: Christianity being true; Moslem, Hindu, Indian, etc. as examples of FALSE.

It is clear that in the minds of our Founding Fathers that Christianity was understood to be a given when the topic "religion" was discussed in America.   If you were to be asked what *"religion"* you were it was synonymous with being asked what Christian denomination you were.

Consider this excerpt from a letter written to the Protestant Episcopal Church by President George Washington on August 19, 1789:   "*It affords edifying prospects, indeed, to see Christians of different denominations dwell together in more charity, and conduct themselves in respect to each other with a more*

Christian-like spirit than ever they have done in any former age, or in any other nation."

Consider the documented wording from drafts made in the Senate on September 3, 1789, pertaining to the construction of the First Amendment:

♦ *"Congress shall not make any law infringing the rights of conscience, or establishing any <u>religious sect</u> or society."*
♦ *"Congress shall make no law establishing any <u>particular denomination</u> of religion in preference to another, or prohibit the free exercise thereof, nor shall the rights of conscience be infringed."*
♦ *"Congress shall make no law establishing <u>one religious society</u> in preference to others, or to infringe on the rights of conscience."*
♦ *"Congress shall make no law <u>establishing religion</u> or prohibiting the free exercise thereof."*
♦ *Finally ratified, "Congress shall make no law respecting <u>an establishment of religion</u>, or prohibiting the free exercise thereof."*

Remember, the colonists were 98% Protestant. They were considered very progressive in every state to offer full rights as citizens to all Christian denominations. Many people today try to reinterpret exactly what the intent was of our Founding Fathers. **But consider this report in the United States Congress received of Mr. Meacham of the House Committee on the Judiciary on March 27, 1854.** Remember also that these men were in many cases the children and grandchildren of those that penned the Constitution.

(Begin Quotation) *"Congress shall make no law respecting an establishment of religion." Does our present practice (employing chaplains) violate that article? ...chaplains were appointed for the Revolutionary army on its organization; rules for their regulation are found among the earliest of the articles of war.* Congress ordered, on May 27, 1777, that there should be one chaplain to each brigade of the army, nominated by the brigadier-general, and appointed by Congress, with the same pay as colonel...The American Congress began its session September 5, 1774. On the second day of the session, Mr. Samuel Adams proposed to open the session with prayer.

I give Mr. Webster's account of it:

> *"At the meeting of the first Congress there was a doubt in the minds of many about the propriety of opening the session with prayer; and the reason assigned was, as here, the great diversity of opinion and religious belief (denominations); until, at last, Mr. Samuel Adams, with his gray hairs hanging about his shoulders, and with an impressive venerableness now seldom to be met with (I suppose owing to different habits), rose in that assembly, and, with the air of a perfect Puritan, said it did not become men professing to be Christian men, who had come together for solemn deliberation in the hour of their extremity, to say there was so wide a difference in their religious belief that they could not, as one man, bow the knee*

in prayer to the Almighty, whose advice and assistance they hoped to obtain; and, Independent as he was, and an enemy to all prelacy as he was known to be, he moved that Rev. Mr. Duche', of the Episcopal Church, should address the throne of grace in prayer. John Adams, in his letter to his wife, says he never saw a more moving spectacle. Mr. Duche' read the Episcopal service of the Church of England; and then, as if moved by the occasion, he broke out into extemporaneous prayer, and those men who were about to resort to force to obtain their rights were moved to tears; and floods of tears, he says, ran down the cheeks of the pacific Quakers, who formed part of that interesting assembly; and, depend upon it, that where there is a spirit of Christianity, there is a spirit which rises above form, above ceremonies, independent of sect (denomination) or creed and the controversies of clashing doctrines."

That same clergyman was afterwards appointed chaplain of the American Congress. He had such an appointment five days after the Declaration of Independence. On December 22, 1776, on December 13, 1784, and on February 29, 1788, it was resolved that two chaplains should be appointed. So far for the old American Congress. I do not deem it out of place to notice one act, of many, to show that Congress was not indifferent to the religious interests of the people; and they were not peculiarly afraid of the charge of uniting Church and State. On the 11th of September 1777, ... Congress voted to instruct the Committee on Commerce to import twenty thousand Bibles from Scotland and Holland into the different ports of the Union. The reason assigned was that the use of the book was so universal and important. Now, what was passing on that day? The army of Washington was fighting the battle of Brandywine; the gallant soldiers of the Revolution were displaying their heroic though unavailing valor; twelve hundred soldiers were stretched in death on that battlefield; Lafayette was bleeding; the booming of the cannon was heard in the hall where Congress was sitting, in the hall from which Congress was soon to be a fugitive. At that important hour Congress was passing an order for importing twenty thousand Bibles: and yet we have never heard that they were charged by their generation of any attempt to unite Church and State, or surpassing their powers to legislate on religious matters.

There was a convention assembled between the old and new forms of government. Considering the character of the men, the work in which they were engaged, and the results of their labors, I think them the most remarkable body of men ever assembled. Benjamin Franklin addressed that body on the subject of employing chaplains; and certainly Franklin will not be accused of fanaticism in religion, or of a wish to unite Church and State. There certainly can be no doubt as to the practice of employing chaplains in deliberative bodies previous to the adoption of the Constitution. We are, then, prepared to see if any change was made in that respect in the new order of affairs.

The first Congress under the Constitution began on the 4th of March, 1789...On the 1st day of May, Washington's first speech was read to the House, and the first business after that speech was the appointment of Dr. Linn as chaplain.

By whom was this plan made? **Three out of six of that joint committee were members of the convention that framed the Constitution. Madison, Ellsworth, and Sherman passed directly from the hall of the convention to the hall of Congress. Did they not know what was constitutional?**

At the adoption of the Constitution, we believe every State - certainly ten of the thirteen - provided as regularly for the support of the Church as for the support of the Government: one, Virginia, had the system of tithes. Down to the Revolution, every colony did sustain religion in some form (denomination). It was deemed peculiarly proper that the religion of liberty should be upheld by a free people. **Had the people, during the Revolution, had a suspicion of any attempt to war against Christianity, that Revolution would have been strangled in its cradle. At the time of the adoption of the Constitution and the amendments, the universal sentiment was that Christianity**

*__should be encouraged, not any one sect__. Any
attempt to level and discard all religion would
have been viewed with universal indignation.
__The object was not to substitute Judaism or
Mohammedanism, or infidelity (atheism), but
to prevent rivalry among sects to the
exclusion of others.... It must be considered
as the foundation on which the whole
structure rests.__*

*Laws will not have permanence or power without
the sanction of religious sentiment, - without a
firm belief that there is a Power above us that will
reward our virtues and punish our vices. __In this
age there can be no substitute for Christianity: that, in its general principles, is the great
conservative element on which we must rely
for the purity and permanence of free
institutions. That was the religion of the
founders of the republic, and they expected it
to remain the religion of their descendants.__
There is a great and very prevalent error on this
subject in the opinion that those who organized
this Government did not legislate on religion."*
(End Quotation)

Of course, Christianity cannot be imposed upon any
man. When one is confronted with his own sinfulness,
presented with the Gospel of Jesus Christ, convicted by
the drawing and convincing of the Holy Spirit – that
person has the choice to either believe or not believe.
That is an act of the conscience. However, our nation
was founded on basic Biblical principles and any who
wish to live in America, as citizens must be willing to
honor and adhere to the Law of the Land.

SECTION 4: Our Biblical Foundation

Knowing that King George III had placed himself above the Law of God, the British Common Law, the Magna Carta, and the English Bill of Rights, the American Colonists (who were British subjects at the time) followed the prescribed remedy for the removal of a tyrannical government. **As the Declaration of Independence was signed, Sam Adams said,** *"We have this day restored the Sovereign to Whom all men ought to be obedient. He reigns in heaven and from the rising to the setting of the sun, let His kingdom come."*

That document stated clearly the basis for this new Nation.

> *When in the Course of human events it becomes necessary for one people to dissolve the political bands which have connected them with another and to assume among the powers of the earth, the separate and equal station* **to which the Laws of Nature and of Nature's God** *entitle them, a decent respect to the opinions of mankind requires that they should declare the causes which impel them to the separation.*

> *We hold these truths to be self-evident, that all men are* **created** *equal, that* **they are endowed by their Creator with certain unalienable Rights, that among these are Life, Liberty and the pursuit of Happiness. — That to secure these rights, Governments are instituted among Men.**

According to Sir William Blackstone, the authority on English Law in his Commentaries on Law: *"Man, considered as a creature, must necessarily be subject to the laws of his Creator, for he is entirely a dependent being ... And consequently, as man depends absolutely upon his Maker for everything, it is necessary that he should in all points conform to his Maker's will. This will of his Maker is called the law of nature...And if our reason were always, as in our first ancestor (Adam) before his transgression, clear and perfect, unruffled by passions, unclouded by prejudice, unimpaired by disease or intemperance, the task would be pleasant and easy; we should need no other guide but this. But every man now finds the contrary in his own experience; that his reason is corrupt, and his understanding full of ignorance and error.*

This has given manifold occasion for the benign interposition of divine providence; which, in compassion to the frailty, the imperfection, and the blindness of human reason, hath been pleased, at sundry times and in divers manners, to discover and enforce it's laws by an immediate and direct revelation. The doctrines thus delivered we call the <u>revealed or divine law, and they are to be found only in the holy scriptures.</u> ...Upon these two foundations, the law of nature and the law of revelation, depend all human laws; that is to say, no human laws should be suffered to contradict these." (Blackstone Commentaries on Law, Book One, Section Two)

The United States of America was established on the Laws of God's nature and recorded for us in the Holy Scriptures. That is the Foundation of America. God alone grants rights and the purpose of government is to secure these rights to man. Notice how the Biblical principals are intricately woven into our governing documents.

Natural Law. Romans 2:14-16 *For when the Gentiles, which have not the law, do by nature the things contained in the law, these, having not the law, are a law unto themselves: Which shew the work of the law written in their hearts, their conscience also bearing witness, and their thoughts the mean while accusing or else excusing one another;) In the day when God shall judge the secrets of men by Jesus Christ according to my gospel.*

Life (Personal Liberty). Genesis 2:7 *And the LORD God formed man of the dust of the ground, and breathed into his nostrils the breath of life; and man became a living soul.*

Liberty (Personal Freedom). Galatians 5:1 *Stand fast therefore in the liberty wherewith Christ hath made us free, and be not entangled again with the yoke of bondage.*

Pursuit of Happiness (Safe to live and work).
To fear/reverence/obey God – Proverbs 28:14;
To work and live life in safety - Ecclesiastes 3:12-13.

*For he has so intimately connected, so
inseparably interwoven <u>the laws of eternal
justice with the happiness of each individual,</u> that
the latter cannot be attained but by observing the
former; and, if the former be punctually obeyed,
it cannot but induce the latter. In consequence of
which mutual connection of justice and human
felicity (happiness), he has not perplexed the law
of nature with a multitude of abstracted rules and
precepts, referring merely to the fitness or
unfitness of things, as some have vainly
surmised; but <u>has graciously reduced the rule of
obedience to this one paternal precept, "that man
should pursue his own true and substantial
happiness.</u>" This is the foundation of what we call
ethics, or natural law.* **(Blackstone: 1, 2)**

The **First Amendment** protected the American Citizen's
rights to *"preach the Gospel"* (Mark 16:15) and to *"not to
forsake the assembling of yourselves together."*
(Hebrews 10:25) Therefore, those God given rights of
peaceable assembly, worship freely, the freedom of
speech, and the freedom of the press were granted.

The **Second Amendment** protects the American
citizen's right to keep and bear arms, as taken from
Luke 11:21, where Jesus said, *"When a strong man
armed keepeth his palace, his goods are in peace."*

The **Fourth Amendment** that protects a person's property from unreasonable search and seizure is referenced in Deut 24:10-11 *"When thou dost lend thy brother any thing, thou shalt not go into his house to fetch his pledge. Thou shalt stand abroad, and the man to whom thou dost lend shall bring out the pledge abroad unto thee."*

The **Eighth Amendment** that protects from "cruel and unusual punishment" is a scriptural mandate where the punishment is to fit the crime. *(Eye for eye, tooth for tooth).*

Our three **branches of government** are patterned after the three positional offices of Christ as found in *Isaiah 33:22. For the LORD is our judge, the LORD is our lawgiver, the LORD is our king; he will save us.* (Judicial, Legislative, Executive)

Representation based upon population numbers (House of Representatives) is found in Deut 1:15 *So I took the chief of your tribes, wise men, and known, and made them heads over you, captains over thousands, and captains over hundreds, and captains over fifties, and captains over tens, and officers among your tribes.*

Equal representation by state is found in Numbers 1:4-5 *And with you there shall be a man of every tribe; every one head of the house of his fathers. And these are the names of the men that shall stand with you.*

Even though one may choose not to accept Christ as his personal Lord and Savior, as an American citizen that person is still bound to follow the laws of this land which were established on Biblical principles. An attack on Christianity was considered to be an attack on the foundation of our Nation.

In the case, **People v. Ruggles, New York Supreme Court, 1811**, the defendant was arrested, charged and convicted for blaspheming Jesus Christ. Consider this finding by the court: *"Christianity in its enlarged sense, as a religion revealed and taught in the Bible, is part and parcel of the law of the land."*

The rendering further mentioned that the same sanctity did not hold for *"the religion of Mohamet and the Grand Lama...and for this plain reason, that we are a Christian people, and the morality of the county is deeply engrafted upon Christianity, and not upon the doctrines or worship of these imposters."*

Consider another attack upon the foundation of America (Christianity) in the **Massachusetts Supreme Court case, Commonwealth v. Abner Kneeland, 1838**. The defendant published defamatory remarks about Christianity. **The court ruled that** *"The First Amendment embraces all who believe in the existence of God, as well...as Christians of every denomination...This provision does not extend to atheists, because they do not believe in God or religion; and therefore...their sentiments and professions, whatever they may be, cannot be called religious sentiments and professions."*

These decisions sound harsh in our politically correct world, but these are the "memorial stones" of our Republic.

Notice, that these dissenters were not put to death. They were not beheaded, impaled, or forced to live as slaves. They were free to live in America. They were free to worship or not worship as they pleased. However, they had to respect the laws of this land, which were founded on the *"Laws of Nature and Nature's God."*

SECTION 5: The Threat of Islam to Our Republic

Adolph Hitler's Minister of Propaganda Joseph Goebbels was quoted to say, *"If the lie is big enough and told often enough, it will be believed."* We are victims of this Orwellian scheme.

So, do you really believe that our Founding Fathers had Islam on their minds when Article VI was written in 1787?

Let's remember some facts:

1. **There WAS a test in every State Constitution at the time of the penning of the Constitution.**

   Consider for example Pennsylvania: *"And each member, before he takes his seat shall make and subscribe the following declaration, viz: "I do believe in one God, the Creator and Governor of the Universe, the Rewarder of the good and Punisher of the wicked. And I do acknowledge the Scriptures of the Old and New Testament to given by Divine Inspiration. And no further or other religious test shall ever hereafter be required of any civil officer of magistrate in this State."*

There was a religious test, administered by each state. You had to believe in the God of the Bible and the inerrancy of the Holy Scriptures. That was the test. How else could you be trusted to govern a nation established upon the *"Laws of Nature and Nature's God"*?

But there was <u>no further test administered by the Federal Government</u> regarding your denomination of Christianity. Your denomination could not be held against you.

2. **Noah Webster, in his 1828 dictionary, specifically identified Islam as a "false religion."**

3. **The New York Supreme Court specifically differentiated between Christianity and Islam as not having equal emphasis in America calling Islam an "imposter" religion.**

4. **Islamic nations were attacking American shipping and enslaving American sailors at the same time the Constitution was being written and ratified.** In 1784, America diplomats John Adams, Ben Franklin and Thomas Jefferson were first sent to negotiate with the Muslim terrorists who were ransacking America's shipping in the Mediterranean Sea. By 1786, Adams and Jefferson candidly asked the Ambassador from Tripoli the motivation behind their unprovoked attacks against Americans. The ambassador said:

    "it was founded on the laws of their Prophet (Mohammed) – it was written in their Koran that all nations who should not have acknowledged their authority were sinners and that it was their right and duty to make war upon them wherever they could be found and to make slaves of all they could take as prisoners; and that every Muslim who should be slain in battle was sure to go to Paradise."

By the time Jefferson was elected President a navy had been built and the decision was made that the *"best way to ensure peace"* with the terrorist nations was *"through the medium of war."* The Battle of Tripoli, forever remembered in the Hymn of the Marine Corps, brought to an end this first American War with Islamic terrorism.

Do you really believe that this enemy religion of America in 1787 was what our Constitutional Convention had in mind as they were drafting Article 6?

SECTION 6: The Solution

In recent months, there have been a number of articles coming out of Europe noting the many complaints among the Muslim population in their countries. The complaints are that the Constitutions of those European nations are not compatible with Sharia Law.

No kidding. Neither is the United States Constitution. One will have to go.

The solution is not one of "political correctness." The bleeding hearts will clamor that these steps are "intolerant" and "unjust." Hogwash. Why aren't those bleeding hearts condemning Turkey for the brutal murders and beheadings of three young Christian men in April of 2007? What was their crime? *They were Christians.*

In order to win the war on terror:

1. **Recognize who we are.** We are, in fact, a nation founded by Patriotic Bible believing Christians with a Republic established on Biblical principles. This recognition would include the dismissal of Islamic chaplains in our military. It is not a question of where their loyalty lies, but when they will act. The Koran is not compatible with our Constitution.

2. **Recognize who the enemy is.** There is good and evil. There are good guys and bad guys. We are the good guys and the Islamic terrorists are the bad guys.

- In fundamental Christianity, we are instructed to preach the Word unto all the World and leave the results up to the Holy Spirit.

- In fundamental Islam, they are mandated to bring the entire world under the authority of Sharia Law. All will be forcibly converted, enslaved or die. There is a big difference.

3. **Send in Missionaries and air evangelistic programming via satellite into these war torn countries.** The battle we are waging is a 'spiritual warfare.' We see the consequences of spiritual warfare every day - in the drunk tanks, VD clinics, drug treatment centers, divorce courts, etc - and in this case we see the results of this spiritual warfare as terrorists strap bombs to their sons and daughters to kill infidels. They need the liberty found only in Christ Jesus.

4. **We need to cut the finances of the "bad guys."** Freeze their accounts; encourage American businesses and brokerages not to do business with radical regimes. We must work diligently to develop other sources of energy and/or other sources for our energy. I find it very hard to believe that America went from the horse and buggy to landing on the moon in 70 years, but have made so little progress from our dependency on oil over the last 40.

5. **We must immediately deport those with Radical ties – even if that means CAIR members.**

6. **We must monitor the funding of the Centers**

of Middle Eastern Studies in our universities and the curriculum that is being taught. Since 1975, Saudi Arabia has invested nearly $90 billion dollars around the world spreading their radical Wahhabi doctrine. Much of that has been donated to establish schools of Middle Eastern Studies in American universities, providing the classroom materials and professors while indoctrinating our next generation of leadership with an Islamic Worldview.

7. **We must secure our borders.** Poor Mexicans aren't the only ones coming across our borders.

8. **Eliminate the access to our prisons by Imams.** Our prisons are a breeding grounds for minorities who have a score to settle with "the man" and feel empowered by the religion of Islam. In order to do this, we must get past step #1.

9. **We are fighting a terrorist mindset in Iraq and Afghanistan. Death has not been viewed as a deterrent, but the martyr believes his own death as the pathway to heaven.** History has shown where past Islamic attacks have been suppressed by the fear of being shot with bullets laced with pig fat or the bodies of the dead defiled by contact with a pig's skin or entrails. As twisted as that thinking appears to the modern mind, any deterrent that takes away the zeal for terrorism and martyrdom, should be utilized.

10. **The deterrent during the Cold War was mutually assured destruction.** That is not a deterrent in this battle. We are not fighting a country but an ideology.

It should be known that the use of small nuclear devices or dirty bombs in American cities will not be tolerated. The security of Mecca and Medina may be directly tied to the security afforded to American cities.

What kind of America will our children and grandchildren live in? Our decisions and actions will decide.

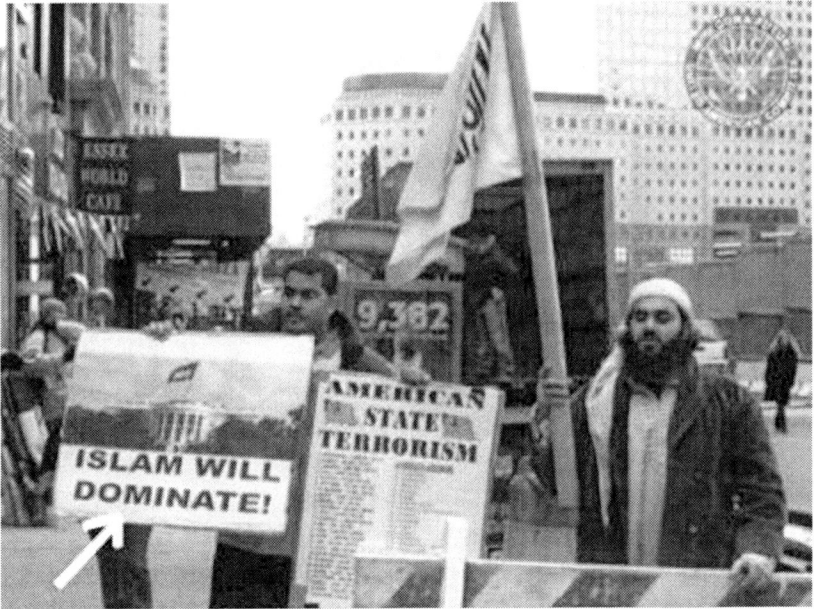

Islamofascist fifth columnists demonstrate against the United American Committee, 1 February 2006. Note their expression of loyalty to the country of which they are supposedly citizens or legal residents.

Source: unitedamericancommittee.org, used by permission at omdurman.org

Special thanks to so many mentors and educators, for the resources used in this essay, including:

The Original 13, Bill Federer
Historical Perspective of a Muslim Being Sworn into Congress, by David Barton
Blackstone's Commentaries on the Law
Library of Congress
Webster's 1828 Dictionary
Mirriam Webster's Modern Dictionary
Myth of Separation, David Barton
America's God and Country, Bill Federer
Backfired, Bill Federer
Chuck Baldwin
Holy Bible, King James Edition

Appendix A

The Declaration of Independence

IN CONGRESS, JULY 4, 1776
The unanimous Declaration of the thirteen United States of America

When in the Course of human events it becomes necessary for one people to dissolve the political bands which have connected them with another and to assume among the powers of the earth, the separate and equal station to which the Laws of Nature and of Nature's God entitle them, a decent respect to the opinions of mankind requires that they should declare the causes which impel them to the separation.

We hold these truths to be self-evident, that all men are created equal, that they are endowed by their Creator with certain unalienable Rights, that among these are Life, Liberty and the pursuit of Happiness. — That to secure these rights, Governments are instituted among Men, deriving their just powers from the consent of the governed, — That whenever any Form of Government becomes destructive of these ends, it is the Right of the People to alter or to abolish it, and to institute new Government, laying its foundation on such principles and organizing its powers in such form, as to them shall seem most likely to effect their Safety and Happiness. Prudence, indeed, will dictate that Governments long established should not be changed for light and transient causes; and accordingly all experience hath shewn that mankind are more disposed to suffer, while evils are sufferable than to right themselves by abolishing the forms to which they are accustomed. But when a long train of abuses and usurpations, pursuing invariably the same Object evinces a design to reduce them under absolute Despotism, it is their right, it is their duty, to throw off such Government, and to provide new Guards for their future security. — Such has been the patient sufferance of these Colonies; and such is now the necessity which constrains them to alter their former Systems of Government. The history of the present King of Great Britain is a history of repeated injuries and usurpations, all having in direct object the establishment of an absolute Tyranny over these States. To prove this, let Facts be submitted to a candid world.

He has refused his Assent to Laws, the most wholesome and necessary for the public good.

He has forbidden his Governors to pass Laws of immediate and pressing importance, unless suspended in their operation till his Assent should be obtained; and when so suspended, he has utterly neglected to attend to them.

He has refused to pass other Laws for the accommodation of large districts of people, unless those people would relinquish the right of Representation in the Legislature, a right inestimable to them and formidable to tyrants only.

He has called together legislative bodies at places unusual, uncomfortable, and distant from the depository of their Public Records, for the sole purpose of fatiguing them into compliance with his measures.

He has dissolved Representative Houses repeatedly, for opposing with manly firmness his invasions on the rights of the people.

He has refused for a long time, after such dissolutions, to cause others to be elected, whereby the Legislative Powers, incapable of Annihilation, have returned to the People at large for their exercise; the State remaining in the mean time exposed to all the dangers of invasion from without, and convulsions within.

He has endeavoured to prevent the population of these States; for that purpose obstructing the Laws for Naturalization of Foreigners; refusing to pass others to encourage their migrations hither, and raising the conditions of new Appropriations of Lands.

He has obstructed the Administration of Justice by refusing his Assent to Laws for establishing Judiciary Powers.

He has made Judges dependent on his Will alone for the tenure of their offices, and the amount and payment of their salaries.

He has erected a multitude of New Offices, and sent hither swarms of Officers to harass our people and eat out their substance.

He has kept among us, in times of peace, Standing Armies without the Consent of our legislatures.

He has affected to render the Military independent of and superior to the Civil Power.

He has combined with others to subject us to a jurisdiction foreign to our constitution, and unacknowledged by our laws; giving his Assent to their Acts of pretended Legislation:

For quartering large bodies of armed troops among us:

For protecting them, by a mock Trial from punishment for any Murders which they should commit on the Inhabitants of these States:

For cutting off our Trade with all parts of the world:

For imposing Taxes on us without our Consent:

For depriving us in many cases, of the benefit of Trial by Jury:

For transporting us beyond Seas to be tried for pretended offences:

For abolishing the free System of English Laws in a neighbouring Province, establishing therein an Arbitrary government, and enlarging its Boundaries so as to render it at once an example and fit instrument for introducing the same absolute rule into these Colonies.

For taking away our Charters, abolishing our most valuable Laws and altering fundamentally the Forms of our Governments:

For suspending our own Legislatures, and declaring themselves invested with power to legislate for us in all cases whatsoever.

He has abdicated Government here, by declaring us out of his Protection and waging War against us.

He has plundered our seas, ravaged our coasts, burnt our towns, and destroyed the lives of our people.

He is at this time transporting large Armies of foreign Mercenaries to compleat the works of death, desolation, and tyranny, already begun with circumstances of Cruelty & Perfidy scarcely paralleled in the most barbarous ages, and totally unworthy the Head of a civilized nation.

He has constrained our fellow Citizens taken Captive on the high Seas to bear Arms against their Country, to become the executioners of their friends and Brethren, or to fall themselves by their Hands.

He has excited domestic insurrections amongst us, and has endeavoured to bring on the inhabitants of our frontiers, the merciless Indian Savages whose known rule of warfare, is an undistinguished destruction of all ages, sexes and conditions.

In every stage of these Oppressions We have Petitioned for Redress in the most humble terms: Our repeated Petitions have been answered only by repeated injury. A Prince, whose character is thus marked by every act which may define a Tyrant, is unfit to be the ruler of a free people.

Nor have We been wanting in attentions to our British brethren. We have warned them from time to time of attempts by their legislature to extend an unwarrantable jurisdiction over us. We have reminded them of the circumstances of our emigration and settlement here. We have appealed to their native justice and magnanimity, and we have conjured them by the ties of our common kindred to disavow these usurpations, which would inevitably interrupt our connections and correspondence. They too have been deaf to the voice of justice and of consanguinity. We must, therefore, acquiesce in the necessity, which denounces our Separation, and hold them, as we hold the rest of mankind, Enemies in War, in Peace Friends.

We, therefore, the Representatives of the united States of America, in General Congress, Assembled, appealing to the Supreme Judge of the world for the rectitude of our intentions, do, in the Name, and by Authority of the good People of these Colonies, solemnly publish and declare, That these united Colonies are, and of Right ought to be Free and Independent States, that they are Absolved from all Allegiance to the British Crown, and that all political connection between them and the State of Great Britain, is and ought to be totally dissolved; and that as Free and Independent States, they have full Power to levy War, conclude Peace, contract Alliances, establish Commerce, and to do all other Acts and Things which Independent States may of right do. — And for the support of this Declaration, with a firm reliance on the protection of Divine Providence, we mutually pledge to each other our Lives, our Fortunes, and our sacred Honor.

— John Hancock

New Hampshire:
Josiah Bartlett, William Whipple, Matthew Thornton

Massachusetts:
John Hancock, Samuel Adams, John Adams, Robert Treat Paine, Elbridge Gerry

Rhode Island:
Stephen Hopkins, William Ellery

Connecticut:
Roger Sherman, Samuel Huntington, William Williams, Oliver Wolcott

New York:
William Floyd, Philip Livingston, Francis Lewis, Lewis Morris

New Jersey:
Richard Stockton, John Witherspoon, Francis Hopkinson, John Hart, Abraham Clark

Pennsylvania:
Robert Morris, Benjamin Rush, Benjamin Franklin, John Morton,
George Clymer, James Smith, George Taylor, James Wilson,
George Ross

Delaware:
Caesar Rodney, George Read, Thomas McKean

Maryland:
Samuel Chase, William Paca, Thomas Stone, Charles Carroll of
Carrollton

Virginia:
George Wythe, Richard Henry Lee, Thomas Jefferson, Benjamin
Harrison, Thomas Nelson, Jr., Francis Lightfoot Lee, Carter
Braxton

North Carolina:
William Hooper, Joseph Hewes, John Penn

South Carolina:
Edward Rutledge, Thomas Heyward, Jr., Thomas Lynch, Jr.,
Arthur Middleton

Georgia:
Button Gwinnett, Lyman Hall, George Walton

The Constitution of the United States

Preamble
We the People of the United States, in Order to form a more perfect Union, establish Justice, insure domestic Tranquility, provide
for the common defence, promote the general Welfare, and secure
the Blessings of Liberty to ourselves and our Posterity, do ordain
and establish this Constitution for the United States of America.

Article. I. - The Legislative Branch
Section 1 - The Legislature
All legislative Powers herein granted shall be vested in a Congress
of the United States, which shall consist of a Senate and House of
Representatives.
Section 2 - The House
The House of Representatives shall be composed of Members
chosen every second Year by the People of the several States, and
the Electors in each State shall have the Qualifications requisite
for Electors of the most numerous Branch of the State Legislature.
No Person shall be a Representative who shall not have attained to
the Age of twenty five Years, and been seven Years a Citizen of
the United States, and who shall not, when elected, be an
Inhabitant of that State in which he shall be chosen.
(Representatives and direct Taxes shall be apportioned among the
several States which may be included within this Union, according
to their respective Numbers, which shall be determined by adding
to the whole Number of free Persons, including those bound to
Service for a Term of Years, and excluding Indians not taxed,
three fifths of all other Persons.) (The previous sentence in parentheses was modified by the 14th Amendment, section 2.) The
actual Enumeration shall be made within three Years after the first
Meeting of the Congress of the United States, and within every
subsequent Term of ten Years, in such Manner as they shall by
Law direct. The Number of Representatives shall not exceed one
for every thirty Thousand, but each State shall have at Least one
Representative; and until such enumeration shall be made, the
State of New Hampshire shall be entitled to chuse(sic) three,

41

Massachusetts eight, Rhode Island and Providence Plantations one, Connecticut five, New York six, New Jersey four, Pennsylvania eight, Delaware one, Maryland six, Virginia ten, North Carolina five, South Carolina five and Georgia three.

When vacancies happen in the Representation from any State, the Executive Authority thereof shall issue Writs of Election to fill such Vacancies.The House of Representatives shall chuse(sic) their Speaker and other Officers; and shall have the sole Power of Impeachment.

Section 3 - The Senate

The Senate of the United States shall be composed of two Senators from each State, (chosen by the Legislature thereof,) (The preceding words in parentheses superseded by 17th Amendment, section 1.) for six Years; and each Senator shall have one Vote.

Immediately after they shall be assembled in Consequence of the first Election, they shall be divided as equally as may be into three Classes. The Seats of the Senators of the first Class shall be vacated at the Expiration of the second Year, of the second Class at the Expiration of the fourth Year, and of the third Class at the Expiration of the sixth Year, so that one third may be chosen every second Year; (and if Vacancies happen by Resignation, or otherwise, during the Recess of the Legislature of any State, the Executive thereof may make temporary Appointments until the next Meeting of the Legislature, which shall then fill such Vacancies.) (The preceding words in parentheses were superseded by the 17th Amendment, section 2.)

No person shall be a Senator who shall not have attained to the Age of thirty Years, and been nine Years a Citizen of the United States, and who shall not, when elected, be an Inhabitant of that State for which he shall be chosen.

The Vice President of the United States shall be President of the Senate, but shall have no Vote, unless they be equally divided.

The Senate shall chuse their other Officers, and also a President pro tempore, in the absence of the Vice President, or when he shall exercise the Office of President of the United States.

The Senate shall have the sole Power to try all Impeachments. When sitting for that Purpose, they shall be on Oath or Affirmation. When the President of the United States is tried, the Chief Justice shall preside: And no Person shall be convicted without the Concurrence of two thirds of the Members present.

Judgment in Cases of Impeachment shall not extend further than to removal from Office, and disqualification to hold and enjoy any Office of honor, Trust or Profit under the United States: but the Party convicted shall nevertheless be liable and subject to Indictment, Trial, Judgment and Punishment, according to Law.

Section 4 - Elections, Meetings

The Times, Places and Manner of holding Elections for Senators and Representatives, shall be prescribed in each State by the Legislature thereof; but the Congress may at any time by Law make or alter such Regulations, except as to the Place of Chusing Senators. The Congress shall assemble at least once in every Year, and such Meeting shall (be on the first Monday in December,) (The preceding words in parentheses were superseded by the 20th Amendment, section 2.) unless they shall by Law appoint a different Day.

Section 5 - Membership, Rules, Journals, Adjournment

Each House shall be the Judge of the Elections, Returns and Qualifications of its own Members, and a Majority of each shall constitute a Quorum to do Business; but a smaller number may adjourn from day to day, and may be authorized to compel the Attendance of absent Members, in such Manner, and under such Penalties as each House may provide.

Each House may determine the Rules of its Proceedings, punish its Members for disorderly Behavior, and, with the Concurrence of two-thirds, expel a Member.

Each House shall keep a Journal of its Proceedings, and from time to time publish the same, excepting such Parts as may in their Judgment require Secrecy; and the Yeas and Nays of the Members of either House on any question shall, at the Desire of one fifth of those Present, be entered on the Journal.

Neither House, during the Session of Congress, shall, without the Consent of the other, adjourn for more than three days, nor to any other Place than that in which the two Houses shall be sitting.

Section 6 - Compensation

(The Senators and Representatives shall receive a Compensation for their Services, to be ascertained by Law, and paid out of the Treasury of the United States.) (The preceding words in parentheses were modified by the 27th Amendment.) They shall in all Cases, except Treason, Felony and Breach of the Peace, be privileged from Arrest during their Attendance at the Session of their respective Houses, and in going to and returning from the same;

and for any Speech or Debate in either House, they shall not be questioned in any other Place.

No Senator or Representative shall, during the Time for which he was elected, be appointed to any civil Office under the Authority of the United States which shall have been created, or the Emoluments whereof shall have been increased during such time; and no Person holding any Office under the United States, shall be a Member of either House during his Continuance in Office.

Section 7 - Revenue Bills, Legislative Process, Presidential Veto

All bills for raising Revenue shall originate in the House of Representatives; but the Senate may propose or concur with Amendments as on other Bills.

Every Bill which shall have passed the House of Representatives and the Senate, shall, before it become a Law, be presented to the President of the United States; If he approve he shall sign it, but if not he shall return it, with his Objections to that House in which it shall have originated, who shall enter the Objections at large on their Journal, and proceed to reconsider it. If after such Reconsideration two thirds of that House shall agree to pass the Bill, it shall be sent, together with the Objections, to the other House, by which it shall likewise be reconsidered, and if approved by two thirds of that House, it shall become a Law. But in all such Cases the Votes of both Houses shall be determined by Yeas and Nays, and the Names of the Persons voting for and against the Bill shall be entered on the Journal of each House respectively. If any Bill shall not be returned by the President within ten Days (Sundays excepted) after it shall have been presented to him, the Same shall be a Law, in like Manner as if he had signed it, unless the Congress by their Adjournment prevent its Return, in which Case it shall not be a Law.

Every Order, Resolution, or Vote to which the Concurrence of the Senate and House of Representatives may be necessary (except on a question of Adjournment) shall be presented to the President of the United States; and before the Same shall take Effect, shall be approved by him, or being disapproved by him, shall be repassed by two thirds of the Senate and House of Representatives, according to the Rules and Limitations prescribed in the Case of a Bill.

Section 8 - Powers of Congress

The Congress shall have Power To lay and collect Taxes, Duties, Imposts and Excises, to pay the Debts and provide for the common Defence and general Welfare of the United States; but all Duties, Imposts and Excises shall be uniform throughout the United States;

To borrow money on the credit of the United States;

To regulate Commerce with foreign Nations, and among the several States, and with the Indian Tribes;

To establish an uniform Rule of Naturalization, and uniform Laws on the subject of Bankruptcies throughout the United States;

To coin Money, regulate the Value thereof, and of foreign Coin, and fix the Standard of Weights and Measures;

To provide for the Punishment of counterfeiting the Securities and current Coin of the United States;

To establish Post Offices and Post Roads;

To promote the Progress of Science and useful Arts, by securing for limited Times to Authors and Inventors the exclusive Right to their respective Writings and Discoveries;

To constitute Tribunals inferior to the supreme Court;

To define and punish Piracies and Felonies committed on the high Seas, and Offenses against the Law of Nations;

To declare War, grant Letters of Marque and Reprisal, and make Rules concerning Captures on Land and Water;

To raise and support Armies, but no Appropriation of Money to that Use shall be for a longer Term than two Years;

To provide and maintain a Navy;

To make Rules for the Government and Regulation of the land and naval Forces;

To provide for calling forth the Militia to execute the Laws of the Union, suppress Insurrections and repel Invasions;

To provide for organizing, arming, and disciplining the Militia, and for governing such Part of them as may be employed in the Service of the United States, reserving to the States respectively, the Appointment of the Officers, and the Authority of training the Militia according to the discipline prescribed by Congress;

To exercise exclusive Legislation in all Cases whatsoever, over such District (not exceeding ten Miles square) as may, by Cession of particular States, and the acceptance of Congress, become the Seat of the Government of the United States, and to exercise like

45

Authority over all Places purchased by the Consent of the Legislature of the State in which the Same shall be, for the Erection of Forts, Magazines, Arsenals, dock-Yards, and other needful Buildings; And To make all Laws which shall be necessary and proper for carrying into Execution the foregoing Powers, and all other Powers vested by this Constitution in the Government of the United States, or in any Department or Officer thereof.

Section 9 - Limits on Congress

The Migration or Importation of such Persons as any of the States now existing shall think proper to admit, shall not be prohibited by the Congress prior to the Year one thousand eight hundred and eight, but a tax or duty may be imposed on such Importation, not exceeding ten dollars for each Person.

The privilege of the Writ of Habeas Corpus shall not be suspended, unless when in Cases of Rebellion or Invasion the public Safety may require it.

No Bill of Attainder or ex post facto Law shall be passed.

(No capitation, or other direct, Tax shall be laid, unless in Proportion to the Census or Enumeration herein before directed to be taken.)

(Section in parentheses clarified by the 16th Amendment.)

No Tax or Duty shall be laid on Articles exported from any State.

No Preference shall be given by any Regulation of Commerce or Revenue to the Ports of one State over those of another: nor shall Vessels bound to, or from, one State, be obliged to enter, clear, or pay Duties in another.

No Money shall be drawn from the Treasury, but in Consequence of Appropriations made by Law; and a regular Statement and Account of the Receipts and Expenditures of all public Money shall be published from time to time.

No Title of Nobility shall be granted by the United States: And no Person holding any Office of Profit or Trust under them, shall, without the Consent of the Congress, accept of any present, Emolument, Office, or Title, of any kind whatever, from any King, Prince or foreign State.

Section 10 - Powers prohibited of States

No State shall enter into any Treaty, Alliance, or Confederation; grant Letters of Marque and Reprisal; coin Money; emit Bills of Credit; make any Thing but gold and silver Coin a Tender in Payment of Debts; pass any Bill of Attainder, ex post facto Law, or Law impairing the Obligation of Contracts, or grant any Title of Nobility.

No State shall, without the Consent of the Congress, lay any Imposts or Duties on Imports or Exports, except what may be absolutely necessary for executing it's inspection Laws: and the net Produce of all Duties and Imposts, laid by any State on Imports or Exports, shall be for the Use of the Treasury of the United States; and all such Laws shall be subject to the Revision and Control of the Congress.

No State shall, without the Consent of Congress, lay any duty of Tonnage, keep Troops, or Ships of War in time of Peace, enter into any Agreement or Compact with another State, or with a foreign Power, or engage in War, unless actually invaded, or in such imminent Danger as will not admit of delay.

Article. II. - The Executive Branch

Section 1 - The President

The executive Power shall be vested in a President of the United States of America. He shall hold his Office during the Term of four Years, and, together with the Vice-President chosen for the same Term, be elected, as follows:

Each State shall appoint, in such Manner as the Legislature thereof may direct, a Number of Electors, equal to the whole Number of Senators and Representatives to which the State may be entitled in the Congress: but no Senator or Representative, or Person holding an Office of Trust or Profit under the United States, shall be appointed an Elector.

(The Electors shall meet in their respective States, and vote by Ballot for two persons, of whom one at least shall not lie an Inhabitant of the same State with themselves. And they shall make a List of all the Persons voted for, and of the Number of Votes for each; which List they shall sign and certify, and transmit sealed to the Seat of the Government of the United States, directed to the President of the Senate. The President of the Senate shall, in the Presence of the Senate and House of Representatives, open all the Certificates, and the Votes shall then be counted. The Person having the greatest Number of Votes shall be the President, if such Number be a Majority of the whole Number of Electors appointed; and if there be more than one who have such Majority, and have an equal Number of Votes, then the House of Representatives shall immediately chuse by Ballot one of them for President; and if no Person have a Majority, then from the five highest on the List the said House shall in like Manner chuse the President. But in chusing the President, the Votes shall be taken by States, the Representation from each State having one Vote; a quorum for this Purpose shall consist of a Member or Members from two-thirds of the States, and a Majority of all the States shall be necessary to a Choice. In every Case, after the Choice of the President, the Person having the greatest Number of Votes of the Electors shall be the Vice President. But if there should remain two or more who have equal Votes, the Senate shall chuse from them by Ballot the Vice-President.) (This clause in parentheses was superseded by the 12th Amendment.)

The Congress may determine the Time of chusing the Electors, and the Day on which they shall give their Votes; which Day shall be the same throughout the United States.

No person except a natural born Citizen, or a Citizen of the United States, at the time of the Adoption of this Constitution, shall be eligible to the Office of President; neither shall any Person be eligible to that Office who shall not have attained to the Age of thirty-five Years, and been fourteen Years a Resident within the United States. (In Case of the Removal of the President from Office, or of his Death, Resignation, or Inability to discharge the Powers and Duties of the said Office, the same shall devolve on the Vice President, and the Congress may by Law provide for the Case of Removal, Death, Resignation or Inability, both of the President and Vice President, declaring what Officer shall then act as President, and such Officer shall act accordingly, until the Disability be removed, or a President shall be elected.) (This clause in parentheses has been modified by the 20th and 25th Amendments.) The President shall, at stated Times, receive for his Services, a Compensation, which shall   neither be increased nor diminished during the Period for which he shall have been elected, and he shall not receive within that Period any other Emolument from the United States, or any of them.

Before he enter on the Execution of his Office, he shall take the following Oath or Affirmation: "I do solemnly swear (or affirm) that I will faithfully execute the Office of President of the United States, and will to the best of my Ability, preserve, protect and defend the Constitution of the United States."

Section 2 - Civilian Power over Military, Cabinet, Pardon Power, Appointments

The President shall be Commander in Chief of the Army and Navy of the United States, and of the Militia of the several States, when the Opinion, in writing, of the principal Officer in each of the executive Departments, upon any subject relating to the Duties of their respective Offices, and he shall have Power to Grant Reprieves and Pardons for Offenses against the United States, except in Cases of Impeachment.

He shall have Power, by and with the Advice and Consent of the Senate, to make Treaties, provided two thirds of the Senators present concur; and he shall nominate, and by and with the Advice and Consent of the Senate, shall appoint Ambassadors, other public Ministers and Consuls, Judges of the supreme Court, and all other Officers of the United States, whose Appointments are not herein otherwise provided for, and which shall be established by Law: but the Congress may by Law vest the Appointment of such inferior Officers, as they think proper, in the President alone, in the Courts of Law, or in the Heads of Departments.

The President shall have Power to fill up all Vacancies that may happen during the Recess of the Senate, by granting Commissions which shall expire at the End of their next Session.

Section 3 - State of the Union, Convening Congress

He shall from time to time give to the Congress Information of the State of the Union, and recommend to their Consideration such Measures as he shall judge necessary and expedient; he may, on extraordinary Occasions, convene both Houses, or either of them, and in Case of Disagreement between them, with Respect to the Time of Adjournment, he may adjourn them to such Time as he shall think proper; he shall receive Ambassadors and other public Ministers; he shall take Care that the Laws be faithfully executed, and shall Commission all the Officers of the United States.

Section 4 - Disqualification

The President, Vice President and all civil Officers of the United States, shall be removed from Office on Impeachment for, and Conviction of, Treason, Bribery, or other high Crimes and Misdemeanors.

Article III. - The Judicial Branch

Section 1 - Judicial powers

The judicial Power of the United States, shall be vested in one supreme Court, and in such inferior Courts as the Congress may from time to time ordain and establish. The Judges, both of the supreme and inferior Courts, shall hold their Offices during good Behavior, and shall, at stated Times, receive for their Services a

Compensation which shall not be diminished during their Continuance in Office.

Section 2 - Trial by Jury, Original Jurisdiction, Jury Trials
(The judicial Power shall extend to all Cases, in Law and Equity, arising under this Constitution, the Laws of the United States, and Treaties made, or which shall be made, under their Authority; to all Cases affecting Ambassadors, other public Ministers and Consuls; to all Cases of admiralty and maritime Jurisdiction; to Controversies to which the United States shall be a Party; to Controversies between two or more States; between a State and Citizens of another State; between Citizens of different States; between Citizens of the same State claiming Lands under Grants of different States, and between a State, or the Citizens thereof, and foreign States, Citizens or Subjects.) (This section in parentheses is modified by the 11th Amendment.)

In all Cases affecting Ambassadors, other public Ministers and Consuls, and those in which a State shall be Party, the supreme Court shall have original Jurisdiction. In all the other Cases before mentioned, the supreme Court shall have appellate Jurisdiction, both as to Law and Fact, with such Exceptions, and under such Regulations as the Congress shall make.

The Trial of all Crimes, except in Cases of Impeachment, shall be by Jury; and such Trial shall be held in the State where the said Crimes shall have been committed; but when not committed within any State, the Trial shall be at such Place or Places as the Congress may by Law have directed.

Section 3 - Treason
Treason against the United States, shall consist only in levying War against them, or in adhering to their Enemies, giving them Aid and Comfort. No Person shall be convicted of Treason unless on the Testimony of two Witnesses to the same overt Act, or on Confession in open Court.

The Congress shall have power to declare the Punishment of Treason, but no Attainder of Treason shall work Corruption of Blood, or Forfeiture except during the Life of the Person attainted.

Article. IV. - The States
Section 1 - Each State to Honor all others
Full Faith and Credit shall be given in each State to the public Acts, Records, and judicial Proceedings of every other State. And the

Congress may by general Laws prescribe the Manner in which such Acts, Records and Proceedings shall be proved, and the Effect thereof.

Section 2 - State citizens, Extradition

The Citizens of each State shall be entitled to all Privileges and Immunities of Citizens in the several States.

A Person charged in any State with Treason, Felony, or other Crime, who shall flee from Justice, and be found in another State, shall on demand of the executive Authority of the State from which he fled, be delivered up, to be removed to the State having Jurisdiction of the Crime.

(No Person held to Service or Labour in one State, under the Laws thereof, escaping into another, shall, in Consequence of any Law or Regulation therein, be discharged from such Service or Labour, But shall be delivered up on Claim of the Party to whom such Service or Labour may be due.) (This clause in parentheses is superseded by the 13th Amendment.)

Section 3 - New States

New States may be admitted by the Congress into this Union; but no new States shall be formed or erected within the Jurisdiction of any other State; nor any State be formed by the Junction of two or more States, or parts of States, without the Consent of the Legislatures of the States concerned as well as of the Congress. The Congress shall have Power to dispose of and make all needful Rules and Regulations respecting the Territory or other Property belonging to the United States; and nothing in this Constitution shall be so construed as to Prejudice any Claims of the United States, or of any particular State.

Section 4 - Republican government

The United States shall guarantee to every State in this Union a Republican Form of Government, and shall protect each of them against Invasion; and on Application of the Legislature, or of the Executive (when the Legislature cannot be convened) against domestic Violence.

Article. V. - Amendment

The Congress, whenever two thirds of both Houses shall deem it necessary, shall propose Amendments to this Constitution, or, on the Application of the Legislatures of two thirds of the several States, shall call a Convention for proposing Amendments, which, in either Case, shall be valid to all Intents and Purposes, as part of this Constitution, when ratified by the Legislatures of three fourths of the several States, or by Conventions in three fourths thereof, as the one or the other Mode of Ratification may be proposed by the Congress; Provided that no Amendment which may be made prior to the Year One thousand eight hundred and eight shall in any Manner affect the first and fourth Clauses in the Ninth Section of the first Article; and that no State, without its Consent, shall be deprived of its equal Suffrage in the Senate.

Article. VI. - Debts, Supremacy, Oaths
All Debts contracted and Engagements entered into, before the Adoption of this Constitution, shall be as valid against the United States under this Constitution, as under the Confederation.
This Constitution, and the Laws of the United States which shall be made in Pursuance thereof; and all Treaties made, or which shall be made, under the Authority of the United States, shall be the supreme Law of the Land; and the Judges in every State shall be bound thereby, any Thing in the Constitution or Laws of any State to the Contrary notwithstanding.
The Senators and Representatives before mentioned, and the Members of the several State Legislatures, and all executive and judicial Officers, both of the United States and of the several States, shall be bound by Oath or Affirmation, to support this Constitution; but no religious Test shall ever be required as a Qualification to any Office or public Trust under the United States.

Article. VII. - Ratification
The Ratification of the Conventions of nine States, shall be sufficient for the Establishment of this Constitution between the States so ratifying the Same.

Done in Convention by the Unanimous Consent of the States present the Seventeenth Day of September in the Year of our Lord one thousand seven hundred and Eighty seven and of the Independence of the United States of America the Twelfth. In Witness whereof We have hereunto subscribed our Names:

Go Washington - President and deputy from Virginia

New Hampshire - John Langdon, Nicholas Gilman

Massachusetts - Nathaniel Gorham, Rufus King

Connecticut - Wm Saml Johnson, Roger Sherman

New York - Alexander Hamilton

New Jersey - Wil Livingston, David Brearley, Wm Paterson, Jona. Dayton

Pennsylvania - B Franklin, Thomas Mifflin, Robt Morris, Geo. Clymer, Thos FitzSimons, Jared Ingersoll, James Wilson, Gouv Morris

Delaware - Geo. Read, Gunning Bedford jun, John Dickinson, Richard Bassett, Jaco. Broom

Maryland - James McHenry, Dan of St Tho Jenifer, Danl Carroll

Virginia - John Blair, James Madison Jr.

North Carolina - Wm Blount, Richd Dobbs Spaight, Hu Williamson

South Carolina - J. Rutledge, Charles Cotesworth Pinckney, Charles Pinckney, Pierce Butler

Georgia - William Few, Abr Baldwin

Attest: William Jackson, Secretary

.

The Amendments

The following are the Amendments to the Constitution. The first ten Amendments collectively are commonly known as the Bill of Rights

.

Amendment 1 - Freedom of Religion, Press, Expression. Ratified 12/15/1791.
Congress shall make no law respecting an establishment of religion, or prohibiting the free exercise thereof; or abridging the freedom of speech, or of the press; or the right of the people peaceably to assemble, and to petition the Government for a redress of grievances.

Amendment 2 - Right to Bear Arms. Ratified 12/15/1791.
A well regulated Militia, being necessary to the security of a free State, the right of the people to keep and bear Arms, shall not be infringed.

Amendment 3 - Quartering of Soldiers. Ratified 12/15/1791.
No Soldier shall, in time of peace be quartered in any house, without the consent of the Owner, nor in time of war, but in a manner to be prescribed by law.

Amendment 4 - Search and Seizure. Ratified 12/15/1791.
The right of the people to be secure in their persons, houses, papers, and effects, against unreasonable searches and seizures, shall not be violated, and no Warrants shall issue, but upon probable cause, supported by Oath or affirmation, and particularly describing the place to be searched, and the persons or things to be seized.

Amendment 5 - Trial and Punishment, Compensation for Takings. Ratified 12/15/1791.
No person shall be held to answer for a capital, or otherwise infamous crime, unless on a presentment or indictment of a Grand Jury, except in cases arising in the land or naval forces, or in the Militia, when in actual service in time of War or public danger; nor shall any person be subject for the same offense to be twice put in jeopardy of life or limb; nor shall be compelled in any criminal case to be a witness against himself, nor be deprived of life, liberty, or property, without due process of law; nor shall private property be

taken for public use, without just compensation.

Amendment 6 - Right to Speedy Trial, Confrontation of Witnesses. Ratified 12/15/1791.
In all criminal prosecutions, the accused shall enjoy the right to a speedy and public trial, by an impartial jury of the State and district wherein the crime shall have been committed, which district shall have been previously ascertained by law, and to be informed of the nature and cause of the accusation; to be confronted with the witnesses against him; to have compulsory process for obtaining witnesses in his favor, and to have the Assistance of Counsel for his defence.

Amendment 7 - Trial by Jury in Civil Cases. Ratified 12/15/1791.
In Suits at common law, where the value in controversy shall exceed twenty dollars, the right of trial by jury shall be preserved, and no fact tried by a jury, shall be otherwise re-examined in any Court of the United States, than according to the rules of the common law.

Amendment 8 - Cruel and Unusual Punishment. Ratified 12/15/1791.
Excessive bail shall not be required, nor excessive fines imposed, nor cruel and unusual punishments inflicted.

Amendment 9 - Construction of Constitution. Ratified 12/15/1791.
The enumeration in the Constitution, of certain rights, shall not be construed to deny or disparage others retained by the people.

Amendment 10 - Powers of the States and People. Ratified 12/15/1791.
The powers not delegated to the United States by the Constitution, nor prohibited by it to the States, are reserved to the States respectively, or to the people.

Amendment 11 - Judicial Limits. Ratified 2/7/1795.
The Judicial power of the United States shall not be construed to extend to any suit in law or equity, commenced or prosecuted against one of the United States by Citizens of another State, or by

Citizens or Subjects of any Foreign State.

Amendment 12 - Choosing the President, Vice-President. Ratified 6/15/1804.
The Electors shall meet in their respective states, and vote by ballot for President and Vice-President, one of whom, at least, shall not be an inhabitant of the same state with themselves; they shall name in their ballots the person voted for as President, and in distinct ballots the person voted for as Vice-President, and they shall make distinct lists of all persons voted for as President, and of all persons voted for as Vice-President and of the number of votes for each, which lists they shall sign and certify, and transmit sealed to the seat of the government of the United States, directed to the President of the Senate; The President of the Senate shall, in the presence of the Senate and House of Representatives, open all the certificates and the votes shall then be counted;
The person having the greatest Number of votes for President, shall be the President, if such number be a majority of the whole number of Electors appointed; and if no person have such majority, then from the persons having the highest numbers not exceeding three on the list of those voted for as President, the House of Representatives shall choose immediately, by ballot, the President. But in choosing the President, the votes shall be taken by states, the representation from each state having one vote; a quorum for this purpose shall consist of a member or members from two-thirds of the states, and a majority of all the states shall be necessary to a choice. And if the House of Representatives shall not choose a President whenever the right of choice shall devolve upon them, before the fourth day of March next following, then the   Vice -President shall act as President, as in the case of the death or other constitutional disability of the President.
The person having the greatest number of votes as Vice-President, shall be the Vice-President, if such number be a majority of the whole number of Electors appointed, and if no person have a majority, then from the two highest numbers on the list, the Senate shall choose the Vice-President; a quorum for the purpose shall consist of two-thirds of the whole number of Senators, and a majority of the whole number shall be necessary to a choice. But no person constitutionally ineligible to the office of President shall be eligible to that of Vice-President of the United States.

Amendment 13 - Slavery Abolished. Ratified 12/6/1865.

1. Neither slavery nor involuntary servitude, except as a punishment for crime whereof the party shall have been duly convicted, shall exist within the United States, or any place subject to their jurisdiction.

2. Congress shall have power to enforce this article by appropriate legislation.

Amendment 14 - Citizenship Rights. Ratified 7/9/1868.

1. All persons born or naturalized in the United States, and subject to the jurisdiction thereof, are citizens of the United States and of the State wherein they reside. No State shall make or enforce any law which shall abridge the privileges or immunities of citizens of the United States; nor shall any State deprive any person of life, liberty, or property, without due process of law; nor deny to any person within its jurisdiction the equal protection of the laws.

2. Representatives shall be apportioned among the several States according to their respective numbers, counting the whole number of persons in each State, excluding Indians not taxed. But when the right to vote at any election for the choice of electors for President and Vice-President of the United States, Representatives in Congress, the Executive and Judicial officers of a State, or the members of the Legislature thereof, is denied to any of the male inhabitants of such State, being twenty-one years of age, and citizens of the United States, or in any way abridged, except for participation in rebellion, or other crime, the basis of representation therein shall be reduced in the proportion which the number of such male citizens shall bear to the whole number of male citizens twenty-one years of age in such State.

3. No person shall be a Senator or Representative in Congress, or elector of President and Vice-President, or hold any office, civil or military, under the United States, or under any State, who, having previously taken an oath, as a member of Congress, or as an officer of the United States, or as a member of any State legislature, or as an executive or judicial officer of any State, to support the Constitution of the United States, shall have engaged in insurrection or rebellion against the same, or given aid or comfort to the enemies thereof. But Congress may by a vote of two-thirds of each House, remove such disability.

4. The validity of the public debt of the United States, authorized by law, including debts incurred for payment of pensions and bounties for services in suppressing insurrection or rebellion, shall not be questioned. But neither the United States nor any State shall assume or pay any debt or obligation incurred in aid of insurrection or rebellion against the United States, or any claim for the loss or emancipation of any slave; but all such debts, obligations and claims shall be held illegal and void.
5. The Congress shall have power to enforce, by appropriate legislation, the provisions of this article.

Amendment 15 - Race No Bar to Vote. Ratified 2/3/1870.

1. The right of citizens of the United States to vote shall not be denied or abridged by the United States or by any State on account of race, color, or previous condition of servitude.
2. The Congress shall have power to enforce this article by appropriate legislation.

Amendment 16 - Status of Income Tax Clarified. Ratified 2/3/1913.

The Congress shall have power to lay and collect taxes on incomes, from whatever source derived, without apportionment among the several States, and without regard to any census or enumeration.

Amendment 17 - Senators Elected by Popular Vote. Ratified 4/8/1913.

The Senate of the United States shall be composed of two Senators from each State, elected by the people thereof, for six years; and each Senator shall have one vote. The electors in each State shall have the qualifications requisite for electors of the most numerous branch of the State legislatures.

When vacancies happen in the representation of any State in the Senate, the executive authority of such State shall issue writs of election to fill such vacancies: Provided, That the legislature of any State may empower the executive thereof to make temporary appointments until the people fill the vacancies by election as the legislature may direct.

This amendment shall not be so construed as to affect the election or term of any Senator chosen before it becomes valid as part of the Constitution.

Amendment 18 - Liquor Abolished. Ratified 1/16/1919. Repealed by Amendment 21, 12/5/1933.
1. After one year from the ratification of this article the manufacture, sale, or transportation of intoxicating liquors within, the importation thereof into, or the exportation thereof from the United States and all territory subject to the jurisdiction thereof for beverage purposes is hereby prohibited.
2. The Congress and the several States shall have concurrent power to enforce this article by appropriate legislation.
3. This article shall be inoperative unless it shall have been ratified as an amendment to the Constitution by the legislatures of the several States, as provided in the Constitution, within seven years from the date of the submission hereof to the States by the Congress.

Amendment 19 - Women's Suffrage. Ratified 8/18/1920.
The right of citizens of the United States to vote shall not be denied or abridged by the United States or by any State on account of sex. Congress shall have power to enforce this article by appropriate legislation.

Amendment 20 - Presidential, Congressional Terms. Ratified 1/23/1933.
1. The terms of the President and Vice President shall end at noon on the 20th day of January, and the terms of Senators and Representatives at noon on the 3d day of January, of the years in which such terms would have ended if this article had not been ratified; and the terms of their successors shall then begin.
2. The Congress shall assemble at least once in every year, and such meeting shall begin at noon on the 3d day of January, unless they shall by law appoint a different day.
3. If, at the time fixed for the beginning of the term of the President, the President elect shall have died, the Vice President elect shall become President. If a President shall not have been chosen before the time fixed for the beginning of his term, or if the President elect shall have failed to qualify, then the Vice President elect shall act as President until a President shall have qualified; and the Congress may by law provide for the case wherein neither a President elect nor a Vice President elect shall have qualified, declaring who shall then act as President, or the manner in which one who is to act shall be selected, and such person shall act accordingly until a President or Vice

President shall have qualified.

4. The Congress may by law provide for the case of the death of any of the persons from whom the House of Representatives may choose a President whenever the right of choice shall have devolved upon them, and for the case of the death of any of the persons from whom the Senate may choose a Vice President whenever the right of choice shall have devolved upon them.

5. Sections 1 and 2 shall take effect on the 15th day of October following the ratification of this article.

6. This article shall be inoperative unless it shall have been ratified as an amendment to the Constitution by the legislatures of three-fourths of the several States within seven years from the date of its submission.

Amendment 21 - Amendment 18 Repealed. Ratified 12/5/1933.

1. The eighteenth article of amendment to the Constitution of the United States is hereby repealed.

2. The transportation or importation into any State, Territory, or possession of the United States for delivery or use therein of intoxicating liquors, in violation of the laws thereof, is hereby prohibited.

3. The article shall be inoperative unless it shall have been ratified as an amendment to the Constitution by conventions in the several States, as provided in the Constitution, within seven years from the date of the submission hereof to the States by the Congress.

Amendment 22 - Presidential Term Limits. Ratified 2/27/1951.

1. No person shall be elected to the office of the President more than twice, and no person who has held the office of President, or acted as President, for more than two years of a term to which some other person was elected President shall be elected to the office of the President more than once. But this Article shall not apply to any person holding the office of President, when this Article was proposed by the Congress, and shall not prevent any person who may be holding the office of President, or acting as President, during the term within which this Article becomes operative from holding the office of President or acting as President during the remainder of such term.

2. This article shall be inoperative unless it shall have been ratified as an amendment to the Constitution by the legislatures of three-fourths of the several States within seven years from the date of its submission to the States by the Congress.

Amendment 23 - Presidential Vote for District of Columbia. Ratified 3/29/1961.

1. The District constituting the seat of Government of the United States shall appoint in such manner as the Congress may direct: A number of electors of President and Vice President equal to the whole number of Senators and Representatives in Congress to which the District would be entitled if it were a State, but in no event more than the least populous State; they shall be in addition to those appointed by the States, but they shall be considered, for the purposes of the election of President and Vice President, to be electors appointed by a State; and they shall meet in the District and perform such duties as provided by the twelfth article of amendment.
2. The Congress shall have power to enforce this article by appropriate legislation.

Amendment 24 - Poll Tax Barred. Ratified 1/23/1964.

1. The right of citizens of the United States to vote in any primary or other election for President or Vice President, for electors for President or Vice President, or for Senator or Representative in Congress, shall not be denied or abridged by the United States or any State by reason of failure to pay any poll tax or other tax.
2. The Congress shall have power to enforce this article by appropriate legislation.

Amendment 25 - Presidential Disability and Succession. Ratified 2/10/1967.

1. In case of the removal of the President from office or of his death or resignation, the Vice President shall become President.
2. Whenever there is a vacancy in the office of the Vice President, the President shall nominate a Vice President who shall take office upon confirmation by a majority vote of both Houses of Congress.
3. Whenever the President transmits to the President pro tempore of the Senate and the Speaker of the House of Representatives his written declaration that he is unable to discharge the powers and duties of his office, and until he transmits to them a written declaration to the contrary, such powers and duties shall be discharged by the Vice President as Acting President.
4. Whenever the Vice President and a majority of either the principal officers of the executive departments or of such other body as Congress may by law provide, transmit to the President pro tempore of

the Senate and the Speaker of the House of Representatives their written declaration that the President is unable to discharge the powers and duties of his office, the Vice President shall immediately assume the powers and duties of the office as Acting President.

Thereafter, when the President transmits to the President pro tempore of the Senate and the Speaker of the House of Representatives his written declaration that no inability exists, he shall resume the powers and duties of his office unless the Vice President and a majority of either the principal officers of the executive department or of such other body as Congress may by law provide, transmit within four days to the President pro tempore of the Senate and the Speaker of the House of Representatives their written declaration that the President is unable to discharge the powers and duties of his office. Thereupon Congress shall decide the issue, assembling within forty eight hours for that purpose if not in session. If the Congress, within twenty one days after receipt of the latter written declaration, or, if Congress is not in session, within twenty one days after Congress is required to assemble, determines by two thirds vote of both Houses that the President is unable to discharge the powers and duties of his office, the Vice President shall continue to discharge the same as Acting President; otherwise, the President shall resume the powers and duties of his office.

Amendment 26 - Voting Age Set to 18 Years. Ratified 7/1/1971.
1. The right of citizens of the United States, who are eighteen years of age or older, to vote shall not be denied or abridged by the United States or by any State on account of age.
2. The Congress shall have power to enforce this article by appropriate legislation.

Amendment 27 - Limiting Congressional Pay Increases. Ratified 5/7/1992.
No law, varying the compensation for the services of the Senators and Representatives, shall take effect, until an election of Representatives shall have intervened.

LaVergne, TN USA
05 December 2009
166063LV00002B/2/P